How to Cure

YOUR DOG

By Richard Hession

Published in the UK by
POWERFRESH Limited
Unit 3 Everdon Park
Heartlands Business Park
NN11 8YJ

Telephone   01327 871 777
Facsimile   01327 879 222
E Mail   info@powerfresh.co.uk

Copyright © 2006 Richard Hession
Cover and interior layout by Powerfresh
Cover Design Sanjit Saha

ISBN 10: 1904967523
ISBN 13: 9781904967521

Printed in Malta by Gutenberg Press Ltd

If you would not write it and sign
it, do not say it

Earl Wilson

It is better to debate a question
without settling it than to settle it
without debate

Joseph Foubert

The person who knows <u>how</u> will always have a job. The person who knows <u>why</u> will always be his boss

Carl C. Wood

Many of life's failures are people who did not realise how close they were to success when they gave up

Thomas Edison

I've got all the money I need if I die by four o' clock this afternoon

Henry Youngman

A leader knows what's best to do;
a manager knows how best to do it

Ken Adelman

Bad artist's copy. Great artist's steal

Picasso

Nothing motivates like self-interest

Graeme West

Owe the Bank £1,000 and it's your problem. Owe the Bank £100 million and it's the Banks problem.

J. P. Getty

A leader does not impose a
decision; he moulds one

Nelson Mandela

Not everything that can be counted
counts, not everything that counts
can be counted

Albert Einstein

Knowledge cannot make us all
leaders, but enable us to decide
which leader to follow

Management Digest

Tack is the ability to describe others as they see themselves

Abraham Lincoln

Elbow grease is still the best
lubricant for success

He uses statistics as a drunken man uses lampposts.... for support rather than illumination

Andrew Lang

Along this tree from root to crown,
Ideas flow up, And vetoes down

Peter Drucker

Corporation, n. An ingenious device for obtaining individual profit without individual responsibility

Ambrose Bierce

The meek may inherit the earth -
but not its mineral rights

J. Paul Getty

A competitor is a potential ally

The flash takes the cash!

Sales resistance is the triumph of mind over patter

In the end, all business operations can be reduced to three words: people, product and profits. People come first

Lee Iacocca

It's tough to climb the ladder of success with your nose to the grindstone, your shoulder to the wheel, your eye on the ball and your ear to the ground

Give them quality. That's the best kind of advertising

Milton S. Hershey

There are three kinds of people:
Those who make things happen,
those who wait for things to
happen, and those who wonder
what the hell happened

Sometimes the biggest risk is not taking any

Price Waterhouse

Broke is a temporary state, poor is a state of mind

Larry Hagman

Anyone can have a good idea, it takes someone special to profit from it

Whenever you see a successful
business, someone once made a
courageous decision

Peter Drucker

A banker is a man who lends you an umbrella when the weather is fair, and takes it away from you when it rains

A man without a smiling face must
not open a shop

Chinese Proverb

What is the difference between a taxidermist and a tax collector? The taxidermist takes only your skin

Mark Twain

When you hire people who are smarter than you are, you prove you are smarter than they are

Robert H. Grant

Work expands so as to fill the time available for its completion

C. Northcote Parkinson

Give a man a fish and he eats for a day. But teach a man to fish - and he'll have no further use for you

Marketing Consultant

Good wares make a quick market

Courage and winning - a self perpetuating cycle, just as fear and losing

Felix Severn

Think global - Act local!

Half the money I spend on advertising is wasted, and the trouble is I don't know which half!

John Wanamaker

Insider Trading: stealing too fast

Calvin Trillin

If they ain't happy - don't refund them - charge more to upgrade to something else

Tony Baird

One of the best ways to persuade others is with your ears - by listening to them

Dean Rusk

If it works - do it again - only bigger!

Herbert Wilcox

A way to a person's money is
through their door

Meetings are indispensable when
you don't want to do anything

J. K. Galbraith

Produce simple plans, speak simply and propose big clear targets

Jack Welch

Criticise the action, not the person

The first requisite in running a major corporation, is the ability to pick good people

Lee Iacocca

I trust you completely, but please send cash

Blessed are the young, for they shall inherit the national debt

Herbert Hoover

Money ain't everything, but it's a
hell of a lot better than what comes
second

John Gotti

Don't maximise profits - optimise them, e.g. optimised body temperature is 98.4 F - maximum body temperature is likely to kill you!

There are two kinds of statistics:
the kind you look up, and the kind
you make up

Rex Stout

Witness the statisticians who drowned crossing a river whose average depth was 3 feet

You'll never plough a field by turning it over in your mind

Irish Proverb

The trouble with the profit system
has always been that it was highly
unprofitable to most people

E. B. White

The entrepreneur always searches for change, responds to it, and exploits it as an opportunity

It is a secret worth knowing that lawyers rarely go to law

Moses Crowell

Rome did not create a great empire by having meetings, they did it by beating the opposition

A wise man knows everything - a
shrewd man knows everyone

He who sells on credit has much
business, but little cash

A major reason capable people fail
to advance is that they don't work
well with their colleagues

Lee Iacocca

Nothing great was ever achieved
without enthusiasm

R. W. Emerson

Most people work just hard enough not to get fired, and get paid just enough money not to quit

George Carlin

You get the best out of others
when you give the best of yourself

Harry Firestone

Do not believe you can do today's job with yesterday's methods and be in business tomorrow

Only the meetings they can't start
without you are the one's worth
attending

Swimming with Sharks

When money goes before, all ways
lie open

The things we fear most in organisations - fluctuations, disturbances, imbalances - are the primary sources of creativity

We have morals, not proposals

Contract: an agreement that is binding, only on the weaker party

Frederick Sawyer

Creditors have better memories
than debtors

Remember that time is money

Benjamin Franklin

Errors have been made.
Others will be blamed

In order to get a loan, you must first prove you don't need it

The most difficult part of getting
to the top of the ladder is getting
through the crowd at the bottom

Arch Ward

Doing a job RIGHT the first time gets the job done. Doing the job WRONG gives you job security

Why is a person that handles your money called a 'Broker'?

Peter Kay

Don't borrow or lend, but if you must do one, lend

Josh Billings

It is a socialist idea that making profits is a vice; I consider that the real vice is making losses

Winston Churchill

We should learn from our mistakes, but really study our successes

A verbal agreement isn't worth the paper it's written on

Louis B. Mayer

Don't imitate, innovate

Hugo Boss

Whether you think that you can,
or that you can't, you are usually
right

Henry Ford

Beware of little expenses: a small leak will sink a great ship

Benjamin Franklin

Teamwork... means never having
to take the blame yourself

The man who minds his own business usually has a good one

Leaders are usually the best
connected, not the best qualified

Grint

A good manager is a man who isn't worried about his own career, but rather the careers of those who work for him

Henry S. M. Burns

Working long hours is neither smart nor efficient - besides no one looks good with a brown nose

Felix Severn

In God we trust; all others cash

American Proverb

It's essential to buy into the company values and sell them to everyone else

Jack Welch

You can order other Little books directly from Powerfresh Limited. All at £2.99 each including postage (UK only)

Postage and packing outside the UK: Europe: add 20% of retail price Rest of the world: add 30% of retail price

To order any Powerfresh book please call 01327 871 777
Powerfresh Limited 3 Everdon Park, Heartlands Business Park, Daventry NN11 8YJ